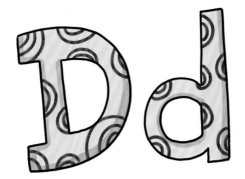 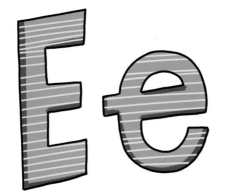 

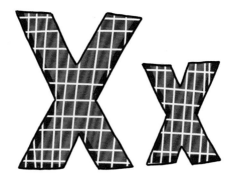 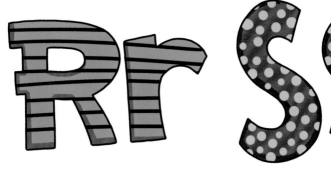  

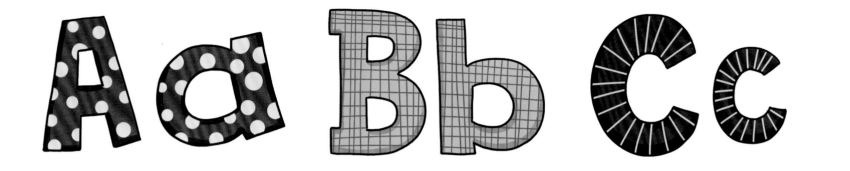

Aa Bb Cc

Gg Hh Ii Jj

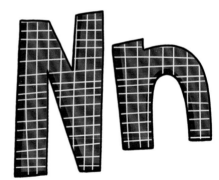

Nn

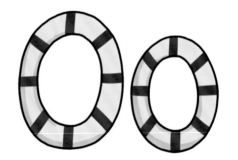

Oo

Pp

Uu

Vv

Ww

This book belongs to

....

First published in 2016 by Miles Kelly Publishing Ltd
Harding's Barn, Bardfield End Green, Thaxted, Essex, CM6 3PX, UK

This edition printed 2017

4 6 8 10 9 7 5

Publishing Director Belinda Gallagher
Creative Director Jo Cowan
Editorial Director Rosie Neave
Managing Designer Joe Jones
Senior Editors Claire Philip, Sarah Parkin
Production Elizabeth Collins, Caroline Kelly
Reprographics Stephan Davis, Jennifer Cozens, Thom Allaway
Assets Lorraine King

ISBN 978-1-78617-014-9

Printed in China

British Library Cataloguing-in-Publication Data
A catalogue record for this book is available from the British Library

ACKNOWLEDGEMENTS
The publishers would like to thank the following artists
who have contributed to this book:
Cover: Hannah Wood at Advocate Art
Advocate Art: Kate Daubney, Ellisamubura, Helen Poole, Hannah Wood
The Bright Agency: Kirsten Collier, Clare Fennell, Maxine Lee, Richard Watson
All other artwork is from the Miles Kelly Artwork Bank

Made with paper from a sustainable forest

www.mileskelly.net

First Dictionary

Miles
Kelly

Contents

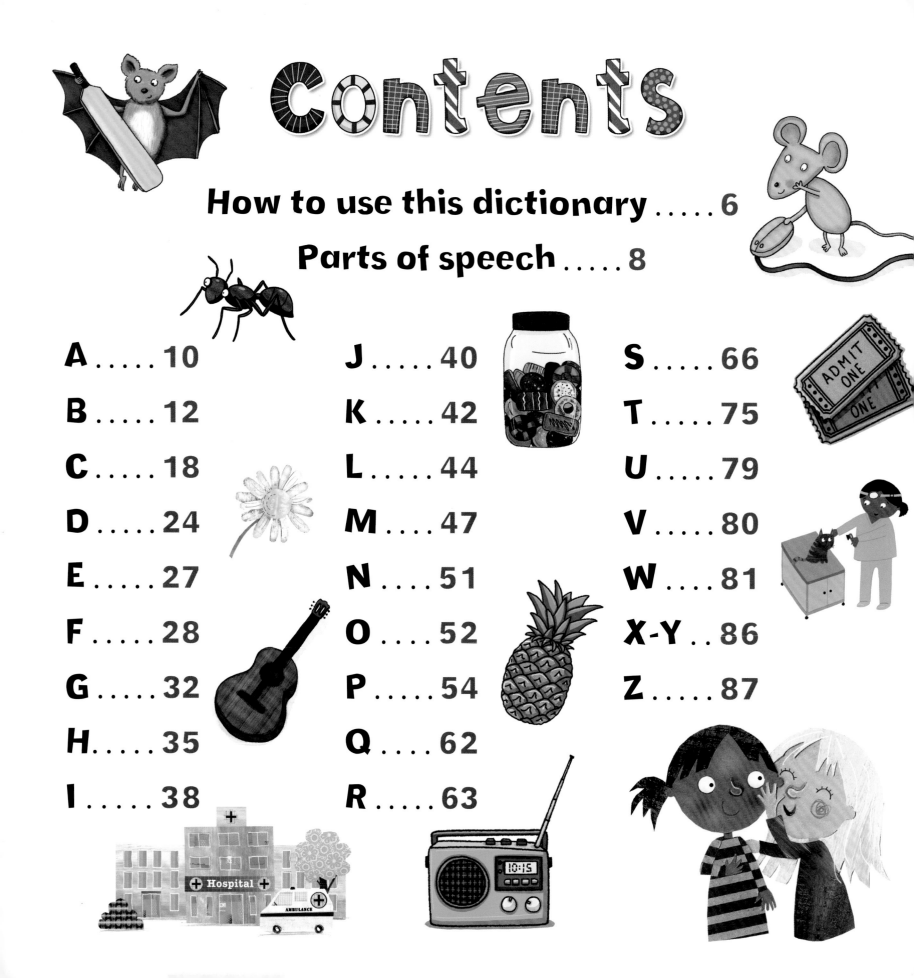

How to use this dictionary 6

Parts of speech 8

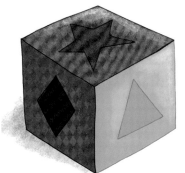

How to use this dictionary

This dictionary explains what words mean and shows you how to spell them correctly.

Alphabet bar

Headwords are organized in alphabetical order, and the alphabet is shown at the side of every page. One letter on the bar is bigger and shown in colour (on page 86 it's two letters). This tells you the first letter of the headwords on that page.

a b c d e f g h i j **k** l m n o p

Kk

kangaroo
A **kangaroo** is an Australian animal that moves by jumping. Females have a pouch on the front of their body, in which they carry their babies.

key
A **key** is a metal object that fits into a lock to open or close a door or box.

kick kicks, kicking, kicked
When you **kick** something, you hit it with your foot.

Finding a word

1. The headwords on each page all begin with the big coloured letter. So if you wanted to find the word **egg**, you would look at the page where **e** is big and coloured.

2. If there are lots of words that all begin with the same letter as the word you are looking for, look next at the second letter in the word and think about alphabetical order again. The second letter of **egg** – **g** – comes after **a** in the alphabet and before **l**, so **egg** comes after **eat** and before **elephant**.

3. If there are more than two words beginning with the same first two letters, you will need to look at the third letter, and so on.

Headwords
The big, bold words are the words that you look up. There are more than 400 in this dictionary.

Entries
Read the definition to find out what a word means. You will find other interesting information here, too.

kiss kisses, kissing, kissed
When you **kiss** someone, you touch them with your lips.

kitten
A **kitten** is a baby cat. Kittens are curious and they love to play.

Parts of speech and plurals
Sometimes extra information is given about a headword – see page 8 for more information.

kite
A **kite** is a toy with a long string that you fly in the wind.

knife
plural: *knives*
A **knife** is a tool with a sharp edge that you use to cut things, and sometimes for spreading.

Word detective
Which of these objects is the odd one out?
doll jigsaw kite vase

43

a b c d e f g h i j **k** l m n o p q r s t u v w x y z

Illustrations
You can also see what a word means by looking at the illustrations. All of the headwords in this dictionary have pictures to illustrate them.

Activity boxes
These will help you learn how to use a dictionary. You can answer the questions in the activity boxes by looking at the entries for those words in the dictionary.

Parts of speech

Words belong to different groups depending on the job they are doing in the sentence or on the information they are giving us. These groups are called parts of speech.

Nouns

A **noun** is a word for a person, animal or a thing, like **table**, **boy** or **mouse**. Most nouns add an **s** to make the plural form: **tables**, **boys**. This dictionary shows you the plural form of nouns that don't follow this rule:

mouse plural: *mice*

One big **mouse** and two small **mice** are eating cheese.

Verbs

A **verb** is a doing word, like **jump**, **sing** and **play**. Verbs have different forms to show who is doing the action, and when they are doing it, and the different forms are given in this dictionary:

sing sings, singing, sang, sung

The girl is **singing** a song. She **sings** beautifully.

8

Adjectives

An **adjective** is a describing word, like **big**, **small**, **happy**, **cold**, and all colours. Most adjectives have an **opposite**.

The cheetah is **fast** and the tortoise is **slow**.

Opposites

big (*large*)	small (*little*)	hot	cold
clean	dirty	long	short
dark	light	new	old
deep	shallow	quiet	loud
easy	hard (*difficult*)	right	left
empty	full	right	wrong
fast (*quick*)	slow	soft	hard
fat	thin	strong	weak
good	bad	tall	short
happy	sad	thick	thin
heavy	light	wet	dry
high	low	young	old

Aa

address plural: *addresses*

Your **address** is the house number, street and town where you live.

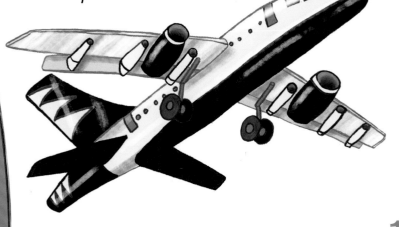

Meadow Lane

aeroplane

An **aeroplane** is a vehicle with wings that flies through the air.

Also: *plane*

airport

An **airport** is a place where aeroplanes land and take off.

alphabet

Our **alphabet** is a list of the letters from A to Z in a special order.

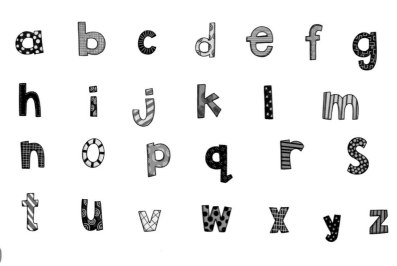

a b c d e f g
h i j k l m
n o p q r s
t u v w x y z

ambulance

An **ambulance** is a vehicle that takes people to hospital.

animal

An **animal** is a living thing that can move. Cats, ants, owls and people are all animals.

ant

An **ant** is a tiny insect that lives with other ants in a group.

apple

An **apple** is a round, crisp fruit.

astronaut

An **astronaut** is a person who goes into space.

axe

An **axe** is a tool for chopping wood.

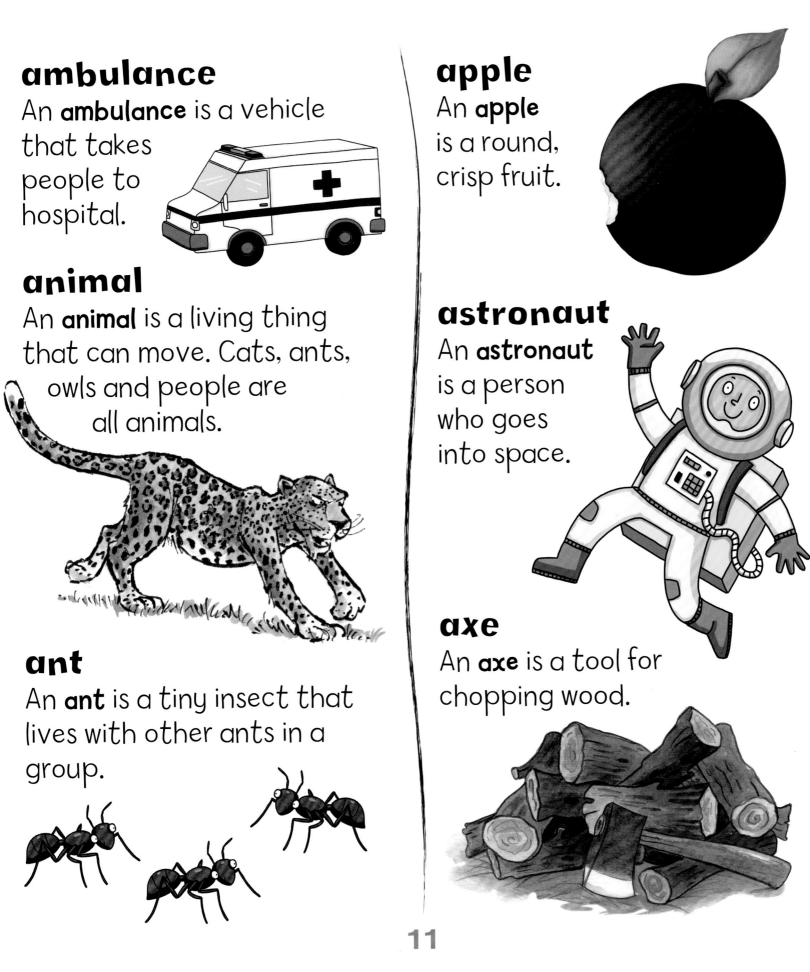

a b c d e f g h i j k l m n o p q r s t u v w x y z

Bb

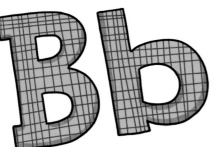

baby
plural: *babies*
A **baby** is a very young child.

ball
A **ball** is a round object that you throw, catch, hit or kick in games.

balloon
A **balloon** is a thin, colourful rubber bag that you can fill with air.

banana
A **banana** is a long, yellow fruit that grows in hot countries.

bat
1. A **bat** is a wooden stick that you use to hit a ball in games.
2. A **bat** is an animal that looks like a mouse, but has wings and can fly.

beach **plural:** *beaches*
A **beach** is an area of sand or pebbles next to the sea.

12

bear

A **bear** is a big, strong, wild animal with thick fur.

bed

A **bed** is a piece of furniture that you sleep on.

bee

A **bee** is a flying insect with black and yellow stripes. Bees make honey.

bell

A **bell** is a metal object that makes a ringing sound.

bicycle

A **bicycle** is a vehicle with two wheels and pedals that you press with your feet.

Also: *bike*

Super sort

Can you put these words in alphabetical order?

peach   orange   banana

b

a
c
d
e
f
g
h
i
j
k
l
m
n
o
p
q
r
s
t
u
v
w
x
y
z

bird

A **bird** is an animal with wings, feathers and a beak.

birthday

Your **birthday** is the day of the year when you were born. Every birthday means you are one year older.

blood

Blood is the red liquid inside you that you see when you cut yourself. Your heart pumps blood around your body.

boat

A **boat** is a small vehicle that moves across water. Boats can carry people and objects.

Lost letters

Which word ends in an x and which ends in a y?
A **bo_** is a male child.
A **bo_** is a four-sided container.

bone

A **bone** is one of the hard, white parts inside your body. All your bones together make up your skeleton.

book

A **book** is a set of pieces of paper inside a cover. Books can have words, or pictures, or both.

bottle

A **bottle** is a tall glass or plastic container for water, milk and other liquids.

box   plural: *boxes*

A **box** is a strong container with four sides and a bottom, and usually with a lid.

boy

A **boy** is a male child. When a boy grows up he becomes a man.

bread

Bread is a common food made of flour.

break breaks, breaking, broke, broken

When something **breaks**, or when you **break** something, it becomes cracked or damaged.

bridge

A **bridge** is like a road over a river or main road for people or vehicles to cross.

brush

plural: *brushes*

A **brush** is an object with bristles or stiff hairs, and a handle.

bubble

A **bubble** is a small ball of air inside a liquid.

bucket

A **bucket** is a round container with a handle. You can use a bucket to carry water.

16

building

A **building** is a place with walls and a roof.

bus

plural: *buses*

A **bus** is a large road vehicle that can carry a lot of people.

butterfly   plural: *butterflies*

A **butterfly** is a flying insect with large, brightly coloured wings.

button

A **button** is a small round object for fastening clothes.

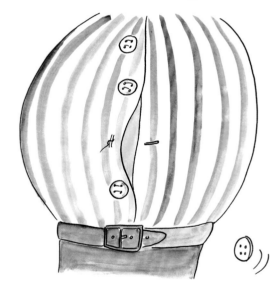

Word detective
Which one of these things is not a liquid?
bubble   milk   water

a
b
c
d
e
f
g
h
i
j
k
l
m
n
o
p
q
r
s
t
u
v
w
x
y
z

Cc

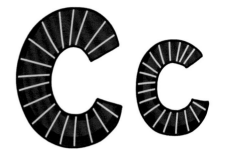

cake

A **cake** is a sweet food made from flour, sugar and eggs.

calf   plural: *calves*

A **calf** is a baby cow.

camel

A **camel** is a large animal with one or two humps on its back. Camels live in the desert.

camera

A **camera** is an object that you use for taking photographs.

candle

A **candle** is a piece of wax with a length of string inside. The string burns slowly to give off light.

car

A **car** is a road vehicle that can carry a few people.

castle

A **castle** is a large building with thick, strong walls.

cat

A **cat** is a furry animal with whiskers, sharp claws and a tail.

caterpillar

A **caterpillar** is a small, often hairy animal that will turn into a butterfly or moth.

chair

A **chair** is a piece of furniture that one person can sit on.

cheese

Cheese is a food made from milk.

19

a b **c** d e f g h i j k l m n o p q r s t u v w x y z

chicken

A **chicken** is a farm bird. It lays eggs that people collect and eat. Meat from this bird is also called chicken.

child plural: *children*

A **child** is a boy or girl, not a grown-up.

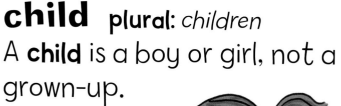

chocolate

Chocolate is a sweet brown or white food made from cocoa beans and sugar.

circus plural: *circuses*

A **circus** is a show in a tent with clowns and acrobats.

climb climbs, climbing, climbed

When you **climb** a mountain or stairs, you go up to the top.

20

clock

A **clock** shows you what time it is.

close closes, closing, closed

When you **close** a door or window, you shut it so that it is no longer open.

cloud

A **cloud** is a white or grey object in the sky. Clouds are made up of tiny drops of water.

clown

A **clown** is a person in funny clothes who makes people laugh. You can see clowns at the circus.

colour

Red, blue and yellow are **colours**. There are many other colours.

Word detective
Which of these animals is the odd one out?
chicken   deer   bear   wolf

a b c d e f g h i j k l m n o p q r s t u v w x y z

computer

A **computer** is a machine that you use to write emails, play games and to use the internet.

cook cooks, cooking, cooked

When you **cook**, you prepare meals by heating up food.

count counts, counting, counted

When you **count** things, you say the numbers in order to find out how many things there are.

cow

A **cow** is a large female farm animal that gives us milk.

crab

A **crab** is a sea animal with large claws and a shell.

crane

A **crane** is a tall machine that lifts very heavy things.

crocodile

A **crocodile** is a large reptile with a long body and tail, short legs, thick scaly skin and sharp teeth.

cry cries, crying, cried

When you **cry**, tears come out of your eyes. People cry when they are sad or hurt.

cup

A **cup** is a container with a handle that you drink from.

cupboard

A **cupboard** is a piece of furniture with doors. You keep things in a cupboard.

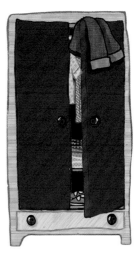

Dd

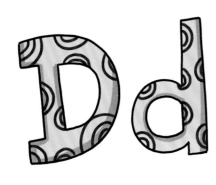

daffodil

A **daffodil** is a yellow flower that grows in spring.

daisy plural: *daisies*

A **daisy** is a small wild flower with white petals around a yellow centre.

dance dances, dancing, danced

When you **dance**, you move your body around while music is playing.

deer

plural: the same

A **deer** is a wild animal. Male deer have long horns called antlers.

dentist

A **dentist** is a person who checks and looks after your teeth.

desert

A **desert** is a very dry place. Not many plants can grow in a desert.

digger

A **digger** is a machine that moves soil and earth.

dinosaur

A **dinosaur** is an animal that lived on land millions of years ago.

doctor

A **doctor** is a person who looks after ill people and helps them get better.

dog

A **dog** is an animal that some people keep as a pet in their home.

Super sort

Can you put these words in alphabetical order?

dog   fox   cat

doll

A **doll** is a toy that looks like a person.

a b c d e f g h i j k l m n o p q r s t u v w x y z

dolphin

A **dolphin** is a large mammal that lives in the sea.

dragon

A **dragon** is a monster with wings in a story. Dragons breathe out fire.

draw draws, drawing, drew, drawn

When you **draw** with a pencil or crayon, you make a picture.

dream dreams, dreaming, dreamt or dreamed

When you **dream**, you see pictures inside your head while you are asleep.

drum

A **drum** is a musical instrument that you hit with a stick or your hand.

duck

A **duck** is a water bird. Ducks have webbed feet, which help them to swim.

26

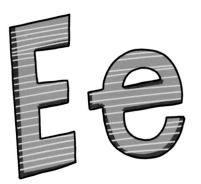

Ee

earring

An **earring** is a piece of jewellery that people can wear in their ears.

earth

Earth is another word for the soil in which plants grow. The name of our planet is Earth.

eat eats, eating, ate, eaten

When you **eat**, you take food into your mouth and swallow it.

egg

An **egg** is a small oval object with a thin shell. Birds, reptiles, fish and insects lay eggs.

elephant

An **elephant** is a very big, wild, grey animal with a long trunk, large ears and two tusks.

envelope

An **envelope** is a paper cover for a letter.

a b c d e f g h i j k l m n o p q r s t u v w x y z

Ff

factory

plural: *factories*

A **factory** is a building where people use machines to make things.

fall   falls, falling, fell, fallen

When something **falls** it drops onto the ground.

family   plural: *families*

A **family** is a group of people who are related to each other, such as a mother, father, sister and brother.

farm

A **farm** is a place with land for growing crops and keeping animals. A person who works on a farm is called a farmer.

favourite

Your **favourite** thing is the thing you like best.

feather

A **feather** is one of the soft, light parts that cover a bird's body.

field

A **field** is a piece of ground with grass growing on it.

finish finishes, finishing, finished

When you **finish** something, you reach the end of it.

fire

A **fire** is hot flames that can be seen when something is burning.

fire engine

A **fire engine** is a vehicle that carries firefighters and their equipment.

firework

A **firework** is a bright, colourful object that a grown-up lights, then it shoots into the sky and explodes.

fish plural: the same

A **fish** is an animal that lives in water. Fish have fins to help them swim.

flag

A **flag** is a piece of cloth with a special design and colours on it. Every country in the world has a different flag.

flour

Flour is a white or brown powder made from wheat. You use flour to make bread and cakes.

flower

A **flower** is the brightly coloured part of a plant.

fly (noun) plural: *flies*

A **fly** is a small insect with wings.

fly (verb) flies, flying, flew, flown

When something **flies**, it moves through the air.

30

forest

A **forest** is a large area of land where a lot of trees grow close together.

fox   plural: *foxes*

A **fox** is a wild animal that looks like a dog. Foxes have bushy tails.

friend

A **friend** is a person you like a lot, but who is not in your family.

frog

A **frog** is a small green animal that lives near water. Frogs jump by using their strong back legs.

fruit

Fruit is the part of a plant with seeds. We eat lots of types of fruits, such as grapes, apples and oranges.

fur

Fur is the soft hair that grows on the skin of some animals.

a b c d e f g h i j k l m n o p q r s t u v w x y z

Gg

game
A **game** is an activity that you play for fun.

garage
A **garage** is a building where people keep a car.

garden
A **garden** is a piece of land with plants next to a house.

gate
A **gate** is a door in a fence or wall.

giant
A **giant** is a very tall person in stories.

giraffe
A **giraffe** is a tall wild animal with a very long neck.

32

girl

A **girl** is a female child who will grow up to be a woman.

glass

1. **Glass** is a hard, see-through material. Windows and mirrors are made of glass.

2. plural: *glasses*
A **glass** is a container made from glass that you drink from.

glasses

Glasses are two pieces of glass in a frame that can help people to see better.

goat

A **goat** is a farm animal with two horns that curve backwards.

goldfish

plural: *the same*
A **goldfish** is a small orange fish that some people keep as a pet.

goose   plural: *geese*

A **goose** is a water bird that looks like a large duck.

a b c d e f g h i j k l m n o p q r s t u v w x y z

gorilla

A **gorilla** is a wild animal that looks like a big monkey with no tail. Gorillas have long arms.

grandparent

Your **grandparents** are the parents of your parents — they are your grandma and grandpa.

grass

Grass is a very common plant that covers the ground, often in parks or gardens.

grow

grows, growing, grew, grown

When something **grows**, it gets bigger.

guitar

A **guitar** is a musical instrument with strings and a long neck. You hold a guitar in front of your stomach when you play it.

Super sort

Can you put these words in alphabetical order?

guitar   violin   piano

Hh

hair
Your **hair** is the soft covering on your head.

half   plural: *halves*
A **half** is one of two equal parts. Two halves make one whole. You can write a half like this: $\frac{1}{2}$

hammer
A **hammer** is a tool that you use to hit nails into wood.

hear   hears, hearing, heard
When you **hear** sounds, they reach your ears and you notice them.

helicopter
A **helicopter** is a flying vehicle with blades on top that spin round.

help   helps, helping, helped
When you **help** someone, you make a job easier for them.

a b c d e f g h i j k l m n o p q r s t u v w x y z

hide hides, hiding, hid

When you **hide** something, you put it somewhere where no one can find it.

hill

A **hill** is a high piece of ground that is not as tall as a mountain.

hole

A **hole** is an opening, gap or empty space in something solid.

holiday

A **holiday** is a time when people do not have to go to school or work.

home

Your **home** is the place where you live.

honey

Honey is a sweet, sticky food that bees make.

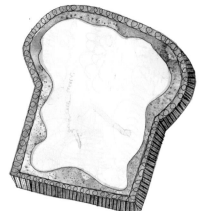

hop hops, hopping, hopped

When you **hop**, you jump up and down on one foot.

horse

A **horse** is a large animal that people can sit on and ride.

hospital

A **hospital** is a big building where people who are sick or hurt go to get better.

house

A **house** is a building where people, often a family, live.

Making sounds
Which three of these letters can be followed by an **h** at the start of a word?
c j s t y

a b c d e f g **h** i j k l m n o p q r s t u v w x y z

Ii

ice

Ice is water that has frozen and become solid. Ice turns back to water when it melts.

ice cream

Ice cream is a very cold, frozen food made from cream and sugar.

igloo

An **igloo** is a house made out of blocks of snow and ice.

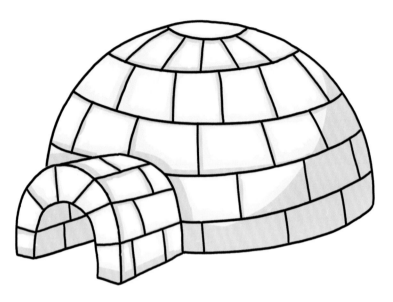

insect

An **insect** is a small animal with six legs. Some insects have wings. Flies, ants and bees are insects.

instrument

An **instrument** is an object that you play to make music.

internet

The **internet** is a huge system that lets computers all over the world send messages to each other.

invite invites, inviting, invited

When you **invite** a person to your house or to your party you ask them to come to it.

island

An **island** is a piece of land with water all around it.

Building words

Can you join each word on the left to the correct word on the right to make three other words?

light   glasses

snow   house

sun   man

Jj

jar

A **jar** is a glass container, in which you can keep food.

jellyfish   plural: the same

A **jellyfish** is a sea animal with a soft body and long arms or legs called tentacles. Some types of jellyfish can sting.

jewellery

Earrings and necklaces are types of **jewellery**. People wear jewellery for decoration.

jigsaw

A **jigsaw** is a puzzle made from pieces of wood or cardboard that fit together to make a picture.

joke

A **joke** is a funny story that makes people laugh.

40

juggle juggles, juggling, juggled

When you **juggle**, you throw two or more objects in the air and catch them quickly. A person who juggles is called a juggler.

juice

Juice is the liquid that can be squeezed out of fruits and vegetables.

jump jumps, jumping, jumped

If you **jump**, you spring into the air by pushing off with your feet.

jungle

A **jungle** is a thick forest in a hot country, where it rains a lot.

a b c d e f g h i j k l m n o p q r s t u v w x y z

Kk

kangaroo

A **kangaroo** is an Australian animal that moves by jumping. Females have a pouch on the front of their body, in which they carry their babies.

kennel

A **kennel** is a little shelter for a dog to sleep in.

key

A **key** is a metal object that fits into a lock to open or close a door or box.

kick kicks, kicking, kicked

When you **kick** something, you hit it with your foot.

king

A **king** is a man who is the leader of a country. A king's wife is usually a queen.

kiss kisses, kissing, kissed

When you **kiss** someone, you touch them with your lips.

kite

A **kite** is a toy with a long string that you fly in the wind.

kitten

A **kitten** is a baby cat. Kittens are curious and they love to play.

knife

plural: *knives*
A **knife** is a tool with a sharp edge that you use to cut things, and sometimes for spreading.

Word detective
Which of these objects is the odd one out?
doll jigsaw kite vase

43

a b c d e f g h i j k l m n o p q r s t u v w x y z

Ll

ladder

A **ladder** is two long poles with short bars between them. Ladders help you climb up to high places.

ladybird

A **ladybird** is a small red insect with black spots.

lamb

A **lamb** is a young sheep. It is also the meat from this animal.

laugh laughs, laughing, laughed

When you **laugh**, you make sounds that show you find something funny.

leaf plural: *leaves*

A **leaf** is a flat, green part of a plant or tree.

lemon

A **lemon** is a yellow fruit with a sour taste.

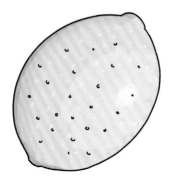

letter

1. A **letter** is one of the signs in the alphabet, such as a, b or c.
2. A **letter** is a message that you write to someone on paper.

library plural: *libraries*

A **library** is a building with a lot of books that you can borrow.

light (noun)

A **light** is an object that is bright and helps you see in the dark.

light (adjective)

1. If something is **light**, it isn't heavy and you can carry it easily.
2. If something is **light** in colour, it is pale and not dark or bright.

lighthouse

A **lighthouse** is a tall tower near the sea with a bright light that flashes to warn ships of danger.

a
b
c
d
e
f
g
h
i
j
k
l
m
n
o
p
q
r
s
t
u
v
w
x
y
z

lightning

Lightning is a bright flash of light in the sky during a thunderstorm.

lion

A **lion** is a large, wild cat. Male lions have long hair, called a mane, on their head and neck.

liquid

A **liquid** is something like water that you can pour.

listen listens, listening, listened

When you **listen**, you use your ears and pay attention to the sounds you can hear.

log

A **log** is a thick piece of wood from a tree trunk.

look looks, looking, looked

When you **look** at something, you use your eyes and pay attention to what you see.

Mm

machine

A **machine** is a piece of equipment, such as a microwave, that uses electricity or an engine to do a job.

magic

Magic is a special power in stories that makes strange or impossible things happen.

magnet

A **magnet** is a piece of metal that pulls other metal objects towards it.

mammal

A **mammal** is a type of animal. Female mammals make milk inside their body to feed their babies. Dogs, tigers, whales and people are mammals.

man   plural: *men*

A **man** is a grown-up boy.

map

A **map** is a drawing of an area. A map shows where places are.

mask

A **mask** is something you wear over your face to hide or protect it.

meat

Meat is the part of an animal that people can eat.

medal

A **medal** is a small piece of metal that people receive for winning a race, or doing something special.

medicine

Medicine is a tablet or liquid that you take when you are ill to help you get better.

mermaid

A **mermaid** is a woman in stories with a fish's tail instead of legs.

48

milk

Milk is a white liquid that female mammals make to feed their babies. The milk in shops is mostly from cows.

mirror

A **mirror** is a special piece of glass, in which you can see yourself.

money

Money is the paper and coins that we use to buy things.

monkey

A **monkey** is an animal with a long tail. Monkeys are good at climbing trees.

monster

A **monster** is a scary animal in stories.

49

a b c d e f g h i j k l m n o p q r s t u v w x y z

moon

The **moon** is the biggest shining object in the sky at night. It moves around our planet Earth.

mud

Mud is soft, wet, sticky soil.

mountain

A **mountain** is a very high and steep hill.

mouse   plural: *mice*

1. A **mouse** is a small furry animal with a long tail.

2. A **mouse** is the part of a computer that you click when you choose things on the screen.

music

Music is the sound you make when you are singing or playing a musical instrument. A person who makes music is called a musician.

Word detective
Which one of these is the name of our planet?
Earth   Moon   X-ray

Nn

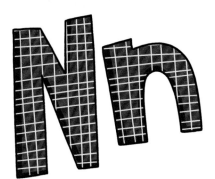

name

A **name** is a word that tells us what people or things are called.

necklace

A **necklace** is a piece of jewellery that you wear around your neck.

nest

A **nest** is a bird's home in a tree. Birds lay eggs in their nest.

noise

A **noise** is a loud sound, or a sound that you don't like.

number

A **number** is a sign that you use when you count. 1, 2 and 3 are numbers.

nurse

A **nurse** is someone whose job it is to care for people who are injured or ill. Nurses often work in hospitals.

nut

A **nut** is a seed with a hard shell.

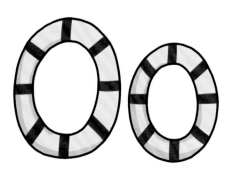

Oo

ocean

An **ocean** is a very big sea between continents.

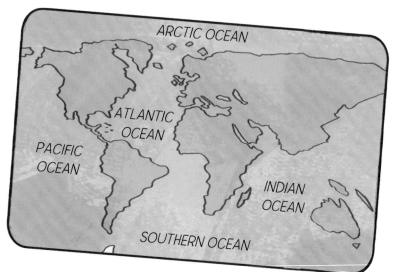

ARCTIC OCEAN

ATLANTIC OCEAN

PACIFIC OCEAN

INDIAN OCEAN

SOUTHERN OCEAN

octopus plural: *octopuses*

An **octopus** is a sea animal with eight arms or legs, called tentacles.

oil

1. **Oil** is a thick liquid from plants that you can use for cooking.

2. **Oil** is a thick liquid deep underground that is used to make petrol.

Oil

onion

An **onion** is a round vegetable with a strong taste and smell. You take off the papery skin before you eat the onion.

open (verb) opens, opening, opened

When you **open** something, you move it so that it is no longer closed.

open (adjective)

When something is **open**, it is not closed.

Word detective

Which one of these things is not a bird?

goose   ladybird   owl

orange (noun)

An **orange** is a round, sweet, juicy fruit with a thick skin.

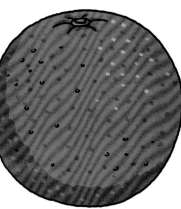

orange (adjective)

Orange is a colour that is a mixture of red and yellow.

ostrich

plural: *ostriches*

An **ostrich** is a very big bird that can run fast but that cannot fly.

owl

An **owl** is a bird with big eyes that hunts for food at night.

a b c d e f g h i j k l m n o p q r s t u v w x y z

Pp

paint (noun)

Paint is a coloured liquid that you use to colour a surface or make pictures.

paint (verb) paints, painting, painted

When you **paint**, you colour something or make pictures with paint.

pair

A **pair** is a set of two things that go together.

panda

A **panda** is a large, furry, black and white bear. Pandas feed mostly on a plant called bamboo.

paper

Paper is a material that you write and draw on.

54

parachute

A **parachute** is a large piece of cloth that helps people fall slowly through the air after they have jumped out of an aeroplane.

parcel

A **parcel** is something wrapped up in paper and tied with string or sticky tape.

parent

A **parent** is a mother or father.

park (noun)

A **park** is an area with grass and trees where people can sit or play.

park (verb) parks, parking, parked

When you **park** a vehicle, you leave it somewhere for a while.

a b c d e f g h i j k l m n o p q r s t u v w x y z

parrot

A **parrot** is a brightly coloured bird. Parrots have strong, hooked beaks.

party   plural: *parties*

A **party** is a time when people meet to have fun and enjoy themselves.

paw

A **paw** is an animal's foot.

pea

A **pea** is a tiny, round, green vegetable that grows in a pod.

peach

plural: *peaches*

A **peach** is a juicy fruit with yellow and red skin and a stone inside.

peacock

A **peacock** is a male bird with brightly coloured tail feathers.

pear

A **pear** is a green or yellow juicy fruit that is narrower at the top than at the bottom.

pebble

A **pebble** is a small, smooth stone on a beach.

pencil

A **pencil** is a small stick of wood with a point that you use to write or draw.

Super sort
Can you put these words in alphabetical order?
pig   parrot   penguin

penguin

A **penguin** is a black and white sea bird. Penguins cannot fly, but they swim using their wings as flippers.

people

People are human beings, or men, women and children. The word people is the plural of the word person, which means one human being.

a
b
c
d
e
f
g
h
i
j
k
l
m
n
o
p
q
r
s
t
u
v
w
x
y
z

pet

A **pet** is an animal that lives with people in their home. Dogs, cats, fish and rabbits are popular pets.

phone (noun)

short for *telephone*

A **phone** is an instrument that you use to talk to someone who is in a different place.

phone (verb)

phoning, phoned, phones

short for *telephone* *telephoning, telephoned, telephones*

When you **phone** someone, you call them on the phone.

photo short

for *photograph*

A **photo** is a picture that you take with a camera.

piano

A **piano** is a large musical instrument with black and white keys.

Word detective

Which one of these is not a person?

parent photo pilot

picnic

A **picnic** is a meal that you eat out of doors, and share with other people.

picture

A **picture** is a drawing, painting or photograph.

pig

A **pig** is a pink or black farm animal with a curly tail.

pilot

A **pilot** is a person who flies an aircraft.

pineapple

A **pineapple** is a large, juicy, yellow fruit with a thick skin and pointed leaves on top.

a b c d e f g h i j k l m n o p q r s t u v w x y z

pirate

A **pirate** is a robber who attacks ships and boats at sea and steals things from them.

planet

A **planet** is a very large round object in space that moves around the Sun. Our planet is called Earth.

plant

A **plant** is a living thing with roots and leaves that grows in soil.

play plays, playing, played

When you **play**, you take part in a game or do something for fun.

police officer

A **police officer** is someone whose job it is to make sure that people do not break the law.

pony
plural: *ponies*

A **pony** is a small horse. Ponies are usually strong.

post office

A **post office** is a shop where you can buy stamps and post letters and parcels.

potato
plural: *potatoes*

A **potato** is a hard, white vegetable that grows underground.

present

A **present** is something that you give to someone, especially on their birthday or at Christmas.

puppet

A **puppet** is a doll that you can make move by pulling strings or putting your hand inside it.

puppy
plural: *puppies*

A **puppy** is a baby dog.

a b c d e f g h i j k l m n o p q r s t u v w x y z

Qq

quarter

A **quarter** is one of four equal parts. Four quarters make one whole. You can write a quarter like this: $\frac{1}{4}$

queen

A **queen** is a woman who is the leader of a country, or the wife of a king. A queen is usually part of a royal family.

question

A **question** is a sentence that you ask someone to find out something.

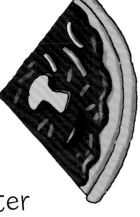

What is your favourite word?

queue

A **queue** is a line of people who are waiting for something.

BUS STOP

Seaside

Rr

rabbit
A **rabbit** is a small furry animal with long ears.

race
A **race** is a competition to find out who is the fastest.

radio
A **radio** is a piece of equipment that receives and sends out sounds.

rain
Rain is water that falls in drops from the sky. When this happens we say that it is raining.

rainbow
A **rainbow** is a curved line in the sky made up of seven colours seen when the sun shines through rain.

read   reads, reading, read
When you **read** a book, you look at the words in it.

63

reptile

A **reptile** is an animal with dry, scaly skin that lays eggs. Snakes, tortoises and lizards are reptiles.

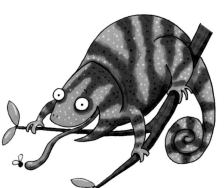

ride rides, riding, rode, ridden

When you **ride** a bike or a horse, you sit on it and make it move.

ring (noun)

A **ring** is a round piece of jewellery that you wear on your finger.

ring (verb)

rings, ringing, rang, rung

1. When something **rings**, it makes a sound like a bell.
2. When you **ring** someone, you phone them.

river

A **river** is a long line of flowing water. Rivers flow into the sea.

road

A **road** is a wide track for vehicles to travel on.

robot

A **robot** is a machine that does jobs that people do. Some robots look like people.

rocket

A **rocket** is a vehicle that burns fuel to travel into space.

rose

A **rose** is a plant with thorns on its stem and flowers that have lots of petals.

run runs, running, ran, run

When you **run**, you move your legs and feet fast to travel over the ground quickly.

Building words

Can you join each word on the left to the correct word on the right to make three other words?

ear	fish
star	flower
sun	ring

a b c d e f g h i j k l m n o p q r s t u v w x y z

Ss

sail (noun)

A **sail** is a large piece of strong cloth fixed to a boat. Sails catch the wind, which makes the boat move.

sail (verb) sails, sailing, sailed

When you **sail**, you travel across water in a boat or ship.

sailor

A **sailor** is a person who works on a boat or a ship as part of the crew.

sand

Sand is made from tiny pieces of rock. It is found on some beaches and in some deserts.

sandwich

plural: *sandwiches*

A **sandwich** is two slices of bread with food in between them.

school

A **school** is a building with classrooms where children go to learn.

scissors

Scissors are a tool with two sharp edges, used to cut paper or cloth.

scooter

A **scooter** is a board on wheels with a handle. You stand on one foot on the board and push along with the other foot.

sea

A **sea** is a large area of salt water.

seal

A **seal** is a mammal that lives in the sea and also on land. Seals have flippers that help them swim.

see sees, seeing, saw, seen

When you **see** something, you look at it or notice it with your eyes.

shadow

Your **shadow** is the dark shape you can see when your body blocks light from reaching the ground.

shark

A **shark** is a large fish with sharp teeth.

sheep

plural: the same
A **sheep** is a farm animal that grows thick wool on its skin.

shell

A **shell** is the hard covering of an egg, nut or some animals.

ship

A **ship** is a very large boat.

shop

A **shop** is a building where you go to buy things.

shout shouts, shouting, shouted

When you **shout**, you speak very loudly.

sing sings, singing, sang, sung

When you **sing**, you make music with your voice.

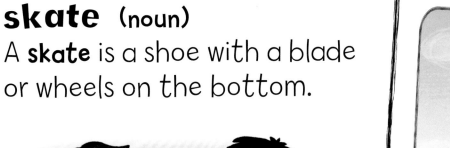

skate (noun)

A **skate** is a shoe with a blade or wheels on the bottom.

skate (verb) skates, skating, skated

When you **skate**, you move across ice or the ground wearing skates.

skeleton

Your **skeleton** is all the bones in your body.

sky

The **sky** is the blue space over our heads.

sleep sleeps, sleeping, slept

When you **sleep**, you close your eyes and rest.

69

a b c d e f g h i j k l m n o p q r S t u v w x y z

smile smiles, smiling, smiled

When you **smile**, your lips curve upwards to show you are happy.

snail

A **snail** is a small animal with a soft body and a shell on its back.

snake

A **snake** is a long, thin reptile with no legs. Snakes have scaly skin.

snow

Snow is tiny flakes of ice that fall from the sky in winter.

snowman

plural: *snowmen*

A **snowman** is a figure made of packed snow that looks like a person.

soldier

A **soldier** is a man or woman in an army.

space

Space is everything a long way above Earth where there is no air. The stars and planets are in space.

spider

A **spider** is a small animal with eight legs that spins webs to catch insects.

squirrel

A **squirrel** is a small, wild, furry animal with a bushy tail.

stamp

A **stamp** is a small piece of paper that you stick on an envelope before you post it.

star

A **star** is a shining point of light in the sky at night.

Lost letters

Which silent letters are missing from these words?

i_land   ha_f   s_issors

a
b
c
d
e
f
g
h
i
j
k
l
m
n
o
p
q
r
S
t
u
v
w
x
y
z

starfish

plural: the same
A **starfish** is a sea animal that is shaped like a star.

start starts, starting, started

When you **start** to do something, you begin to do it.

station

A **station** is a place where trains stop to let people on and off.

strawberry

plural: *strawberries*
A **strawberry** is a small, soft, red fruit with lots of seeds on the outside.

submarine

A **submarine** is a ship that can travel underwater.

sugar

Sugar is a very sweet food that comes from a plant.

suitcase

A **suitcase** is a strong bag that you pack your clothes in when you go on holiday.

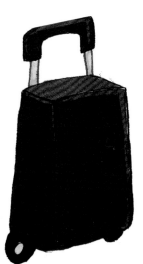

sun

A **sun** is a huge bright star. Our Sun gives our planet heat and light. Earth and seven other planets circle the Sun.

sunflower

A **sunflower** is a tall plant with a big round, yellow flower.

sunglasses

Sunglasses are dark glasses that you wear to protect your eyes when it is very sunny.

supermarket

A **supermarket** is a big shop where you can buy food and other things.

surprise

A **surprise** is something that happens that you didn't expect.

a b c d e f g h i j k l m n o p q r s t u v w x y z

swan

A **swan** is a large white water bird with a long neck.

sweet

If something is **sweet**, it tastes of sugar or honey.

swim swims, swimming, swam, swum

When you **swim**, you use your arms and legs to move through water.

Lost letters

Which of these words needs an **i** to complete it, and which needs an **o**?
A **sh _ p** is a building where you go to buy things.
A **sh _ p** is a very large boat.

swing

A **swing** is a seat that hangs from a bar. When you sit on it, you can move backwards and forwards.

Tt

table

A **table** is a piece of furniture with legs and a flat top.

tadpole

A **tadpole** is a tiny animal that will turn into a frog.

tail

A **tail** is the part of an animal that sticks out at the back of its body. Foxes, squirrels and sharks all have tails.

teacher

A **teacher** is a person who works in a school and helps children learn.

team

A **team** is a group of people who work or play a game with each other.

a b c d e f g h i j k l m n o p q r s t u v w x y z

telephone

A **telephone** is another word for a phone.

telescope

A **telescope** is a long metal tube. When you look through a telescope, it makes objects that are far away look bigger and nearer.

television

A **television** is a machine that shows moving pictures on a screen and sends out sound.

tent

A **tent** is a shelter made of cloth that you can sleep in.

thunder

Thunder is the loud noise you hear during a storm after a flash of lightning.

ticket

A **ticket** is a piece of paper that shows you have paid for a journey on a bus or train or to get into a place.

tiger

A **tiger** is a large, wild cat with orange and black striped fur.

tired

When you are **tired**, you want to sleep or rest.

tomato

plural: *tomatoes*
A **tomato** is a round, red fruit, that can be eaten raw or cooked.

tortoise

A **tortoise** is a reptile with a hard shell covering its body.

toy

A **toy** is an object that you can play with.

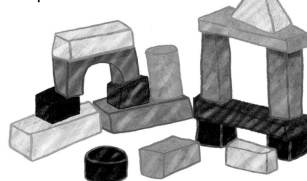

tractor

A **tractor** is a farm vehicle that pulls heavy machines.

train

A **train** is a vehicle with a line of carriages that travels along railway tracks.

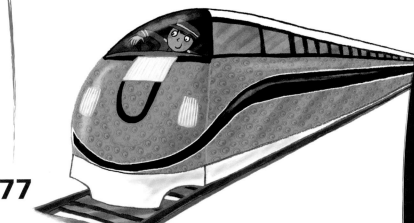

a b c d e f g h i j k l m n o p q r s t u v w x y z

trampoline

A **trampoline** is a large piece of strong cloth fixed to a frame. You bounce up and down on a trampoline.

trapeze

A **trapeze** is a bar hanging from two ropes. People in circuses swing on trapezes.

treasure

Treasure is gold, silver, jewellery and other valuable things.

tree

A **tree** is a tall plant with a trunk, branches and leaves.

trunk

1. A **trunk** is the thick bottom part of a tree.
2. A **trunk** is an elephant's long nose.

tunnel

A **tunnel** is a long underground road or passage.

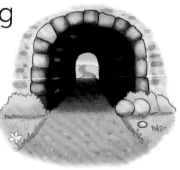

twin

A **twin** is a brother or sister who was born at the same time as you.

Uu

umbrella

An **umbrella** is a piece of material on a frame that you hold over your head to keep yourself dry when it rains.

unicorn

A **unicorn** is an animal in stories that looks like a horse with a horn on its forehead.

uniform

A **uniform** is a special set of clothes that some people in the same school or job wear.

Lost letter
Which letter always follows the letter **q** in words?

a b c d e f g h i j k l m n o p q r s t u v w x y z

Vv

vase

A **vase** is a container for flowers.

vegetable

A **vegetable** is the part of a plant that you can eat.

Word detective

Which one of these objects is not a container?

bottle   jar   ladder   vase

vet

A **vet** is a person trained to treat animals that are ill or injured.

violin

A **violin** is a musical instrument with strings that you hold under your chin and play with a bow.

volcano   plural: *volcanoes*

A **volcano** is a mountain with an opening in the top that sometimes sprays out hot, melted rock.

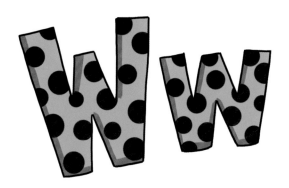

Ww

walk walks, walking, walked

When you **walk**, you put one foot in front of the other and move along the ground.

wash washes, washing, washed

When you **wash** something, you clean it with water.

watch (noun)

plural: *watches*

A **watch** is a small clock that you wear on your wrist.

watch (verb) watches, watching, watched

When you **watch** something, you look at it and pay attention to what you see.

water

Water is a clear liquid that falls from the sky as rain.

wave (noun)

A **wave** is a high line of moving water on the sea.

wave (verb) waves, waving, waved

When you **wave**, you move your hand from side to side to say hello or goodbye.

web

A **web** is a thin net made by a spider. Spiders use webs to trap insects to eat.

whale

A **whale** is a very big sea mammal that breathes through a hole in the top of its head.

wheel

A **wheel** is a round object that turns and makes a vehicle move.

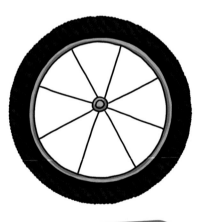

Word detective

Which one of these animals is not a reptile?

crocodile   tortoise
snake   whale

whisper whispers, whispering, whispered

When you **whisper**, you speak very quietly.

whistle

A **whistle** is a small, hollow tube that makes a loud sound when you blow into it.

wind

Wind is air that is moving.

windmill

A **windmill** is a building with long blades, called sails, that turn in the wind.

window

A **window** is an opening in a wall with glass covering it. Windows let in light.

a
b
c
d
e
f
g
h
i
j
k
l
m
n
o
p
q
r
s
t
u
v
w
x
y
z

wing

A **wing** is one of the parts of a bird or insect that moves up and down when it flies. An aeroplane has wings at the side that help it to fly.

witch

plural: *witches*

A **witch** is a person in stories, usually a woman, who has magical powers. Witches are often shown wearing pointy hats.

wizard

A **wizard** is a person in stories, usually a man, who has magical powers.

wolf

plural: *wolves*

A **wolf** is a wild animal that looks like a dog. Wolves hunt in groups called packs.

woman

plural: *women*

A **woman** is a grown-up girl.

wood

Wood is the hard part of a tree. People burn wood to make a fire, or use it to make doors and furniture.

wool

Wool is the thick, soft hair that grows on a sheep's body.

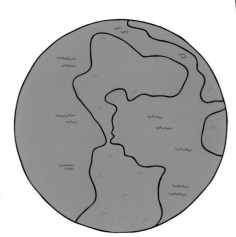

world

The **world** is our planet, and everything that is on it.

worm

A **worm** is a long, thin animal with no legs that lives in the soil.

write writes, writing, wrote, written

When you **write**, you put words on paper with a pen or pencil.

Word detective
Which one of these animals has flippers?
wolf elephant seal

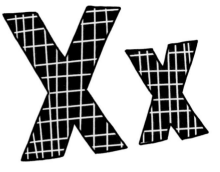

Xx

X-ray

An **X-ray** is a photograph of the inside of your body.

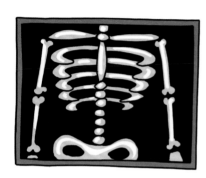

xylophone

A **xylophone** is a musical instrument with a row of wooden bars that you hit with a stick.

Yy

yacht

A **yacht** is a boat with sails.

yawn yawns, yawning, yawned

When you **yawn**, you open your mouth wide and take a big breath. You yawn when you are tired.

yoghurt (or *yogurt*)

Yoghurt is a creamy food made from milk.

yolk

A **yolk** is the yellow part of an egg.

Zz

zebra
A **zebra** is a wild animal with black and white stripes.

zip
A **zip** is a fastener on clothes or bags. It has two lines of teeth that fit together.

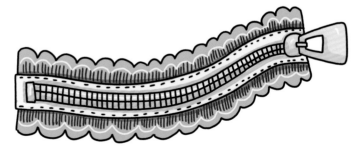

87

Word detective
Which two of these are wild animals?
chicken   dog   squirrel
tiger   goldfish

zoo
A **zoo** is a place where wild animals are kept so that people can go and look at them.

a b c d e f g h i j k l m h o p q r s t u v w x y z

Parts of the body

hair

ear

eye

nose

face

mouth

head

elbow

neck

arm

finger

hand

tummy

knee

leg

ankle

foot

toe

Clothes

vest

sock

pants

skirt

shorts

dress

t-shirt

hat

glove

jacket

scarf

coat

boot

jumper

shirt

trousers

shoe

89

Colours

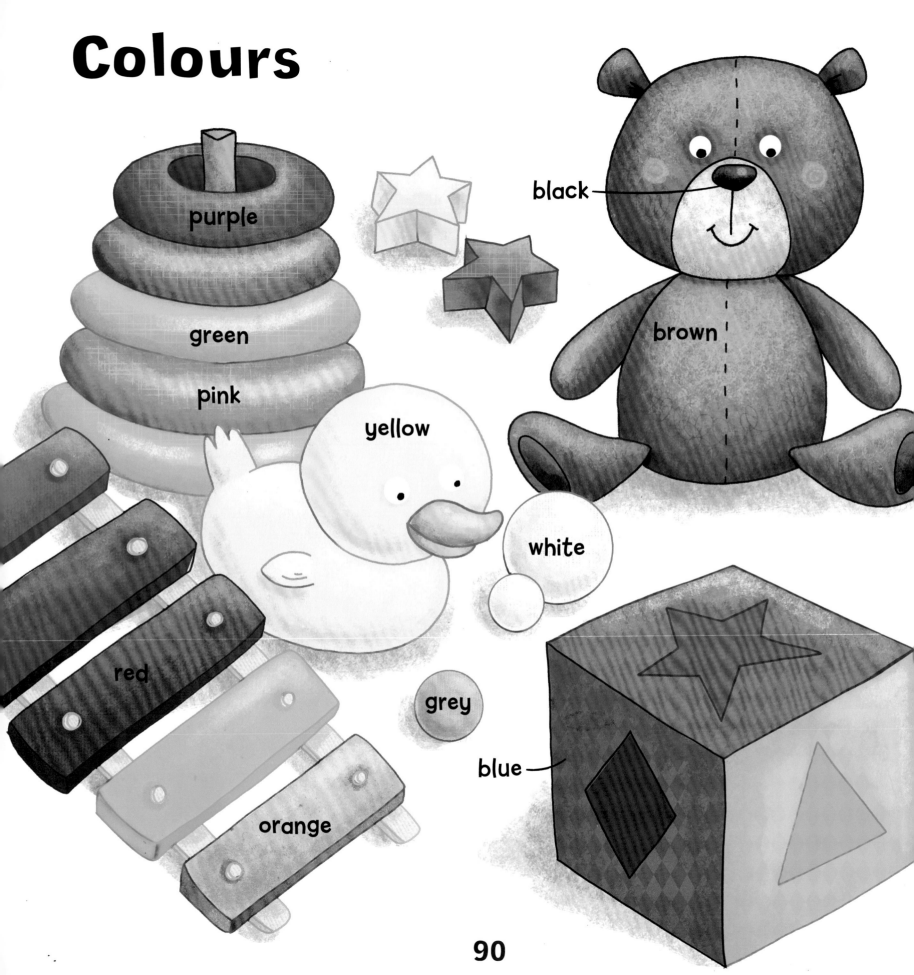

purple

green

pink

yellow

black

brown

white

red

grey

orange

blue

Shapes

circle

star

triangle

semi-circle

diamond

square

rectangle (also: oblong)

hexagon

pentagon

octagon

Question words

Questions that ask for information begin with one of these words: **who**, **what**, **when**, **where**, **which**, **how**, **why** or **whose**.

To ask about a person, begin your question with **who**.
Who is the tallest in the class?

To ask about a thing or an activity, begin your question with **what**.
What are you holding in your hand?

A shell.

It's me, Danny.

To ask about time, begin your question with **when**.
When is your party?

Please come to my
Party
on Saturday

To ask about a place, begin your question with **where**.
Where are you going?

To the supermarket.

To ask about the way you do something, begin your question with **how**.
How do you get to school?

By bus.

To ask about something where you can choose between two or more things, begin your question with **which**.
Which ice cream do you want?

The chocolate one, please.

To ask the reason for something, begin your question with **why**.
Why are you wearing gloves?

Because it's cold outside.

To ask about who something belongs to, begin your question with **whose**.
Whose book is this?

It's Laura's book.

93

Time

Days of the week

Monday

Tuesday

Wednesday

Thursday

Friday

Saturday

Sunday

Months of the year

Days and **months** always begin with a capital letter.

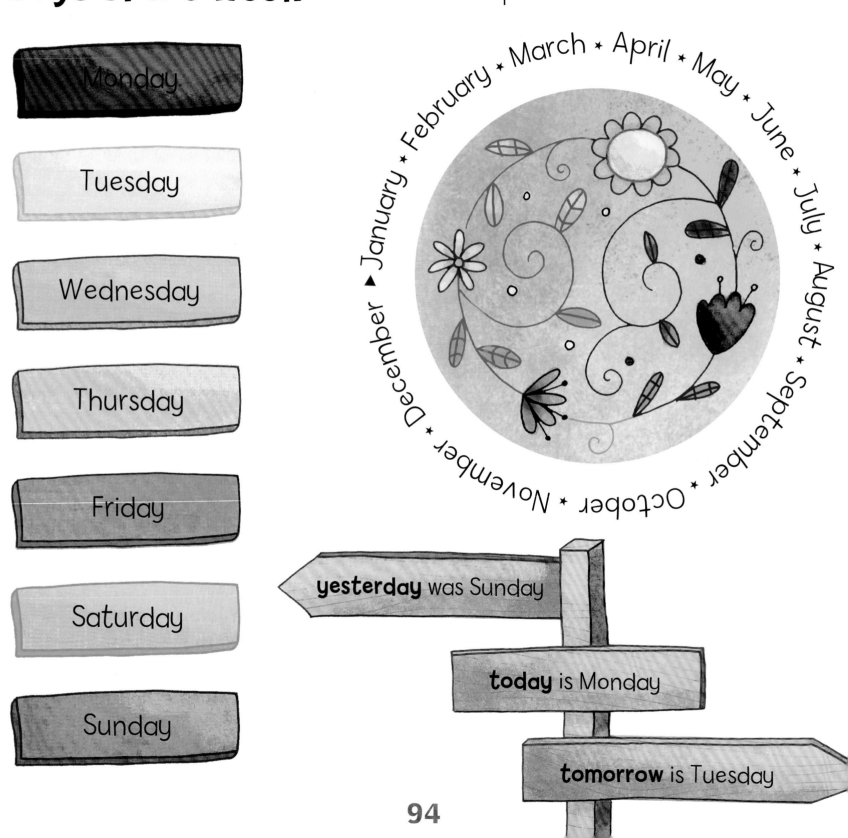

▶ January ✳ February ✳ March ✳ April ✳ May ✳ June ✳ July ✳ August ✳ September ✳ October ✳ November ✳ December ✳

yesterday was Sunday

today is Monday

tomorrow is Tuesday

94

Times of day

morning

afternoon

midday

evening

night

midnight

Telling the time

one **o'clock**

half past
three

**(a) quarter
to** five

**(a) quarter
past** seven

Numbers

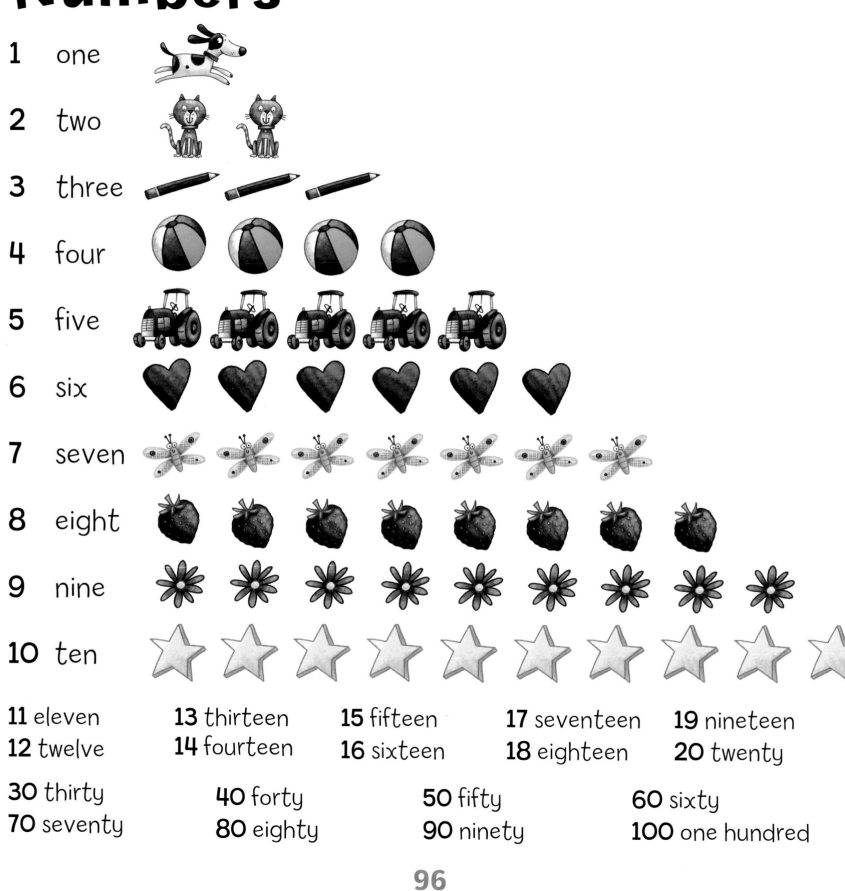

1 one

2 two

3 three

4 four

5 five

6 six

7 seven

8 eight

9 nine

10 ten

11 eleven
12 twelve

13 thirteen
14 fourteen

15 fifteen
16 sixteen

17 seventeen
18 eighteen

19 nineteen
20 twenty

30 thirty
70 seventy

40 forty
80 eighty

50 fifty
90 ninety

60 sixty
100 one hundred

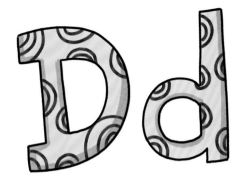  

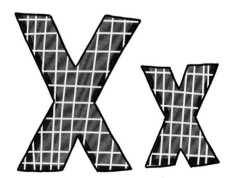  

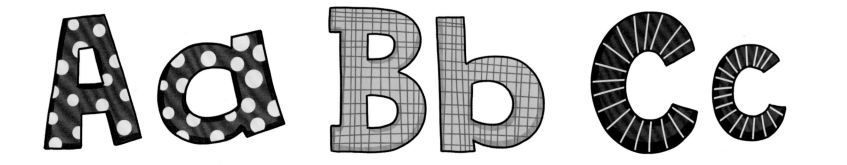

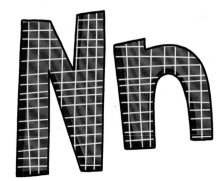

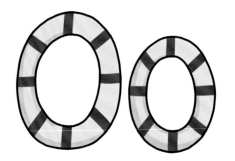

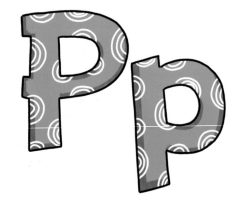